The MINISTRY of Hospitality

The Ministry Of Hospitality
Copyright © 2023 by Dr. Joan A. Polidore

Published in the United States of America
ISBN   Paperback: 979-8-89091-165-0
ISBN   eBook: 979-8-89091-166-7

All rights reserved. No part of this publication may be reproduced, stored in a retrieval system or transmitted in any way by any means, electronic, mechanical, photocopy, recording or otherwise without the prior permission of the author except as provided by USA copyright law.

The opinions expressed by the author are not necessarily those of ReadersMagnet, LLC.

ReadersMagnet, LLC
10620 Treena Street, Suite 230 | San Diego, California, 92131 USA
1. 619. 354. 2643 | www. readersmagnet. com

Book design copyright © 2023 by ReadersMagnet, LLC. All rights reserved.

Cover design by Christian Kedwin Jay Oraiz
Interior design by Daniel Lopez

The MINISTRY of Hospitality

The God of the Bible Wants Us to Treat Each Other with Kindness and Generosity. He also Wants to Heal Us Through Counseling, Reconciliation, and Restoration

Let brotherly love continue. Be not forgetful to entertain strangers: for thereby some have entertained angels unawares.
Hebrews 13:1-2

DR. JOAN A. POLIDORE
Doctorate in Christian Counseling

ReadersMagnet, LLC

TABLE OF CONTENTS

- PREFACE VII
- INTRODUCTION IX
- THE MINISTRY OF HOSPITALITY 1
- THE CHURCH IN THE HOUSE 6
- RESTORATION 7
- THE PLAN AND PURPOSE OF GOD 9
- THE RESULT OF HOSPITALITY THROUGH EVANGELISM 15
- WOMEN MINISTER THROUGH HOSPITALITY 18
- THE SOVEREIGNTY OF GOD THROUGH HOSPITALITY 20
- THE MINISTRY OF THE HOLY SPIRIT-OUR COMFORTER, OUR HELPER 22
- LOVE ACCORDING TO THE BIBLE (KJV) 25
- PRAYER IS THE NUCLEUS OF HOSPITALITY: 29
- HOSPITALITY THROUGH COUNSELING 36
- HOSPITALITY AND KINDNESS 40
- ABOUT THE AUTHOR 49
- ACKNOWLEDGEMENT 53

PREFACE

Hospitality is a ministry consisting of a myriad of ministries within itself. Saving, Healing, Comforting, Restoring, Reconciling, Counseling, and Praying are all inclusive in the Ministry of Hospitality.

After intensive study of this ministry and experiencing its effectiveness, I could not keep all this knowledge to myself. I decided to publish this book with the desire that everyone who reads this book will use this Ministry of Hospitality in whatever area the Lord leads them.

Working with people is not always easy. It is a challenging task which requires much training and constant faith. This book provides you with the biblical knowledge needed to work with people, believing in their complete restoration.

This book describes how God wants us to show kindness and how to be hospitable to those we connect with. It is about connection not perfection; making others feel warm and preparing a welcoming atmosphere in our home. It is about connecting deeply with those we invite into our homes. It is about giving assurance to strangers that are in desperate need of fellowship, restoring those who have been battered and bruised, and giving hope, healing, comfort, restoration, reconciliation and counseling. It is a platform to share Christ's and God's love and saving grace to all who would believe in Him.

This book can be used for small group study, at home, one and one, and also for Women's Ministry in the church. This book neither intends to replace regular, personal Bible study nor is it a replacement for an in-depth study of a particular subject. It is, however, a ministry that the church has lost and needs to regain. I pray that it will be an asset to everyone who reads it and that they will implement it for Kingdom building.

All scriptures are taken from the King James Version of the Bible.

INTRODUCTION

I am one of sixteen children. My childhood was spent in a small village called Morne Prosper, on the Island of Dominica in the Caribbean. The village was called Morne Prosper because it was a prolific mountain. It is noted for its abundance of vegetables, fruits and bananas. As a child, my parents were such devout Roman Catholics, that our home was used as a presbytery for the priests. Their clothes were being washed at the house; they had their meals and rested there as well. The best parts of the vegetables were given to them. As a child, I just could not understand that. My Mother would always cook enough to have leftovers. She would always keep some food for anyone who came by because she said that when people travel, they get hungry and thirsty. At that time, there were no delis for people to buy snacks.

At the age of twenty three, I gave my life over to the Lord completely and began to read the Bible. Only then did I understand what my parents were doing. Now it made sense to me; it was Hospitality. Its real meaning and revelation was life-changing to me. Henceforth, I began to practice it myself, which was very effective in building, restoring, comforting, healing and most of all, preparing people for eternity. I emulated my mother and developed a propensity for Hospitality. To those I connected with, they gravitated towards me and shared their cares and needs. I tried to comfort, give hope, minister healing and soothe their aches and pains.

THE MINISTRY OF HOSPITALITY

Hospitality is a Ministry consisting of a myriad of aspects, Comforting, Restoring, Reconciling, Counseling, and Praying, are all part of the Ministry of Hospitality. The word Hospitality means the same in Latin as hospital. It means hospitable treatment, reception, disposition, a room or suite in a hotel set aside for socializing, or for business purposes (Merriam Webster's College Dictionary).

The Bible meaning of Hospitality in Ministry is to be friendly and welcoming to a guest. This ministry is to encourage and build the Body of Christ. It is to have fellowship with one with another, to give comfort and hope, to restore confidence to those who are in despair, to love unconditionally, to renew and refresh those who have been bruised and battered and to create a welcoming atmosphere for new believers and those who are being saved. As Jesus, said in Isaiah 61:1, "The Spirit of the Lord GOD is upon me; because the Lord hath anointed me to preach good tidings unto the meek; he hath sent me to bind up the brokenhearted, to proclaim liberty to the captives, and the opening of the prison to them that are bound;"

Nevertheless there are many channels on television that entertain the American people, and therefore, the Ministry of Hospitality has been lost in the American Church. Hospitality is all about others; not about you or what you can do. Hospitality is about connecting, making others feel welcome and special, and preparing a comforting atmosphere everywhere we go and at home. It is about building self-esteem and self-worth, restoring and healing as well as connecting deeply with those we meet and invite into our homes. The Power of Hospitality by Cru-na, is to breathe into strangers that are desperately in need of fellowship. It is not about perfection, but connection.

All throughout scripture, we see the Ministry of Hospitality being displayed. The two main purposes of Hospitality are:

a. To share Christ with the lost and to edify the saints
b. For God's purpose to be revealed

The early Church grew because of the House of Fellowship. In 1 John 1:7 it says, "But if we walk in the light, as he is in the light, we have fellowship one with another, and the blood of Jesus Christ his Son cleanseth us from all sin."

The Result of Ananias' Hospitality: Ananias received Paul with gladness and warmth as a beloved brother in the ministry. He was strengthened and encouraged to take up his cross and follow Jesus. "Ananias went his way, and entered into the house; and putting his hands on him said, 'Brother Saul, the Lord, even Jesus that appeared unto thee in the way as thou camest, hath sent me that thou may receive thy sight, and be filled with the Holy Ghost.' And immediately there fell from his eyes as it had been scales: and he received his sight forthwith, and arose, and was baptized. And when he had received meat, he was strengthened. Then was Saul certain days with the disciples which were in Damascus. And straightway he preached Christ in the Synagogues, that he is the Son of God' " (Acts 9:17-19).

Therefore, Paul demonstrated the same gentleness and kindness in his ministry; exhorting believers to be hospitable one to another. "Distributing to the necessity of saints; given to hospitality" (Romans 12:13).

The last thing Jesus did with His disciples was to go into fellowship with them at the "Last Supper". He taught them humility and how to be hospitable to each other through the act of washing their feet. He explained that this act was an example of humble ministry that they must always be ready to perform for one another (John 13:5-17). The woman in Luke 7:44-48 was hospitable to Jesus by washing His feet and drying them with her hair. All she had was a jar of oil and her tears, which she used to anoint Him. What mattered to the woman was to be hospitable to her Savior. She loved much because many sins were forgiven by her Lord Jesus. Hospitality is not how much you have, but it is giving your best to your guest.

The early church was obedient and followed Christ's example in observing the ritual of foot washing: "Well reported of for good works; if she have brought up children, if she have lodged strangers, if she have washed the saints' feet, if she have relieved the afflicted, if she have diligently followed every good work"(1 Timothy 5:10).

Foot washing was an expression of Hospitality extended to guests in biblical times. People traveled dusty roads in Israel and needed to wash their feet for comfort and cleanliness, so foot washing was generally performed by the lowest servant in the household. Guests were often offered water and vessels for washing their own feet (Judges 19:21). At the Last Supper, Jesus washed His disciples' feet and explained that this act was an example of humble ministry that must always be performed by one another (John 13:5-17; 1 Timothy 5:10).

This suggests that the early Church followed Christ's example in observing the ritual of foot washing, but many churches reject this because the other duties mentioned in the verse are household tasks. However, churches of some denominations continue to practice foot washing today.

Here is another example of the church embodying the ministry of Hospitality:

> "And the multitude of them that believed was of one heart and of one soul: neither said any of them that ought of the things which he possessed was his own; but they had all things in common. Neither was there any among them that lacked: for as many as were possessors of lands or houses sold them, and brought the prices of the things that were sold, and laid them down at the apostles' feet: and distribution was made unto every man according as he had need" (Acts 4:32,34-35).

According to the Nelson's Illustrated Bible Dictionary, Hospitality is entertaining strangers graciously. Hospitality was a very important trait in biblical times. In the New Testament, the Greek word for Hospitality literally means love for strangers. In the Old Testament, Abraham entertained angels (Genesis 18:1-15). Even today, a traditional greeting to guests among the Bedouin people of the Middle East is, "You are among your family!" Hospitality was specially commanded by God. "And if a stranger sojourn with thee in the land, ye shall not vex him. But the stranger that dwelleth with you shall be unto you as one born among you, and thou shall love him as thyself; for ye were strangers in the land of Egypt: I am the Lord your God" (Leviticus 19:33-34, Luke 14:13-14, Romans 12:13).

Hospitality was to be the characteristic of all believers (1 Peter 4:9), especially bishops (Titus 1:7-8, (1 Timothy 3:2). Jesus emphasized the importance of Hospitality by answering the question of who should inherit the Kingdom: "....I was a stranger and ye took me in" (Matthew 25:35). Several Old Testament personalities set a good example for all believers in the practice of Hospitality. Psalm 23 concludes with a portrait of a host who prepares a table for the weary, anoints the head of the guest with oil, and shows every kindness so that the guest's cup runs over.

THE CHURCH IN THE HOUSE

The Lord added to the Church daily those who were to be saved, as they fellowshipped in the House. The early Church did not have stained glass windows, equipment, big buildings or technology as we have today, but they cared, loved and shared Jesus with the lost.

The fastest-growing church in the world today is the House Church in China. The disciples taught from house to house which was very effective. The Church in the House broke bread and fellowshipped with each other. They had everything in common. They sold their possessions and goods and divided them among all according to everyone's needs. Hospitality caused them to have favor with all the people and the Lord added to the Church daily such as should be saved (Acts 2:44-47).

Philemon demonstrated love and Hospitality to the brethren in the house church. "I thank my God, making mention of thee always in my prayers. Hearing of thy love and faith which thou hast toward the Lord Jesus, and towards all the saints; That the communication of thy faith may become effectual by the acknowledging of every good thing which is in you in Christ Jesus. For we have great joy and consolation in thy love, because the bowels of the saints are refreshed by thee, brother" (Philemon1:4-7).

RESTORATION

Hospitality is all about refreshing and restoring all others' life through Christ. Paul showed his warmth, love and concern and interceded for the slaves, which had a significant influence on the abolishment of slavery many centuries later. Paul exhorted Philemon to receive his slave back as a beloved brother. Paul promised to pay any expense he incurred. He brought the presence of Christ into the village.

Abraham, our Father of Faith, interceded for Lot and fed strangers (Genesis 18:23-33). We see Abraham and Sarah serving together as they welcome the men who came to their doors. They fed them and refreshed them. They washed the dust off their feet. That is what Hospitality is all about- serving others and refreshing people from their burden of sin. Abraham prepared a young calf for his guests. Hospitality is about giving your best for the Glory of God. Lot and his family were saved through Hospitality. "And Abraham drew near and said, "wilt thou also destroy the righteous with the wicked? Peradventure there be fifty righteous within the city: wilt thou also destroy and not spare the place for the fifty righteous that are therein?" So the Lord went his way as soon as he had finished speaking with Abraham and Abraham returned. There were not even ten righteous in the city but Abraham continued to plead as a compassionate intercessor for the city of Sodom with God. Abraham did not only say "I love my nephew Lot" but he demonstrated that love by his Hospitality to love and intercede on their behalf to God.

THE PLAN AND PURPOSE OF GOD

THE PURPOSE OF GOD BEING FULLFILLED THROUGH HOSPITALITY

"Then the woman took the two men who came to her.... who had entered her house for they had come to search out all the country. So the two men returned, descended from the mountain, and crossed over; and they came to Joshua the son of Nun and told him all that had fallen there...." (Joshua 2:1-23).

Rahab is well-known as a harlot, but her real character is kept a secret to too many. This is a woman of faith and a woman that fears God. She shall be praised. "Favor is deceitful, and beauty is vain: but the woman that feareth the Lord, she shall be praised" (Proverbs 31:30). Rahab was a resourceful woman. She owned the inn.

She was a woman of compassion, a woman of love and warmth. She was a courageous woman. She was a woman longing to be forgiven. Rahab heard about the greatness of the God of Israel and she feared Him. Rahab was not just a bearer of the word but a doer. "And before they were laid down, she came up unto them upon the roof and said unto the men, 'I know that the Lord hath given you the land and that your terror is fallen upon us, and that all the inhabitants of the land faint because of you.

"(Joshua 2:8-9). "For we have heard how the Lord dried up the water of the Red Sea for you, when ye came out of Egypt; and what ye did unto the two kings of the Amorites, that were on the other side of Jordan, Sihon and Og whom ye utterly destroyed" (Joshua 2:10).

Rahab was fully convinced that God had given the land to the children of Israel, therefore she risked her life and took the spies into her house and hid them within the bundles of flax which she had laid on the top of the roof. By doing so, Rahab allowed the purpose of God to come to fruition by being hospitable. Her household was saved and delivered from death and she was included in the genealogy of our Lord and Savior Jesus Christ (Matthew1:5). What Rahab was, was inconsequential to what she became.

The Bible also deals with men in search of God. Many of them are far from being perfect. Among them are those like King David who rose above his wrongdoings and became godly. Even though Rahab was called a harlot, she later became a woman of great faith that could declare to the enemy: The Lord God He is God, the Omnipotent God, the Omniscient God, the Immutable God, "He is God in heaven above and in earth beneath" (Joshua 2:11). The book of Hebrews enrolled Rahab among the faithful along with Sarah. These are the only two women mentioned by name in the famous roll call of the faithful. The harlot Rahab is commended because "By faith the Harlot Rahab perished not with them that believed not, when she had received the spies with peace" (Hebrews 11:31). Rahab also must have been very courageous to be willing to risk her own life to protect the enemy's spies whom she believed to be on an unfriendly mission.

Hospitality is not about you or your house, but about the purpose, plan and will of God to those who are desperately in need of the

Ministry of Hospitality. The Church in America has lost sight of this Ministry.

THE PURPOSE OF GOD BEING FUFILLED THROUGH HOSPITALITY

Older women are called to be hospitable. They should "be in behaviour as becometh holiness, not false accusers, not given to much wine, teachers of good things; that they may teach the young women to be sober, to love their husbands, to love their children, to be discreet, chaste, keepers at home, good, obedient to their own husbands, that the word of God be not blasphemed" (Titus 2:3-5).

The older women must show Hospitality by the life they live. Ruth followed Naomi because of her godly principles and her faith in the "One True God". Mary showed Hospitality through worshipping (Luke 10:40-42). Mary was concerned about heavenly things while her sister, Martha, was concerned about much serving. Many things caught her attention but the only thing that was needful was to spend time with the Lord. The things of the world are attractive and can cause us to lose our focus on Jesus. But Mary stayed focused knowing that the things that are seen are temporal and the things that are not seen are eternal. Therefore, she chose the best by showing her Hospitality through worship.

Naomi taught Ruth how to love and be obedient and respectful to her husband. She was taught how to fear and trust Jehovah God; how to be in love and how to present her body as a living sacrifice, holy and acceptable to God before being married.

The story of Ruth and Boaz is one of the most beautiful love stories of holiness and purity in the Bible. Naomi instructed Ruth on how to present herself for courtship.

"Then Naomi, her mother-in-law said unto her, 'My daughter, shall I not seek rest for thee that it may be well with thee? And now is not Boaz of our kindred, with whose maidens thou wast? Behold he winnoweth barley to night in the threshing floor. Wash thyself therefore, and anoint thee and put thy raiment upon thee, and get thee down to the floor: but make not thyself known unto the man, until he shall have done eating and drinking. And it shall be, when he lieth down, that thou shalt mark the place where he shall lie, and thou shalt go in, and uncover his feet, lay thee down; and he will tell thee what thou shalt do.' And she said unto her, 'All that thou sayest unto me I will do.' And she went down unto the floor, and did according to all that her mother-in-law bade her"(Ruth 3:1-6).

Naomi's love for God motivated Ruth to emulate her and she become Boaz's wife, who bore him a son named Obed, who was the father of Jesse, who was the father of David through whose lineage Jesus came, placing Ruth the Moabitess, who was not of the Commonwealth of Israel, in the genealogy of Jesus Christ.

The sovereign God who loves His people with an everlasting love was watching over Israel before the foundation of the world and brought Jesus into the world through the line of David. "And Jacob begat Joseph, the husband of Mary, of whom was born Jesus, who is called Christ. Now all this was done, that it might be fulfilled which was spoken of the Lord by the prophet, saying, 'Behold, the virgin shall be with child, and shall bring forth a son, and they shall call his name Emmanuel, which being interpreted is, God with us"(Math. 1:16,22-23).

This affirms that Naomi was rewarded for her love for God; the testimony of this godly woman, which she maintained before her daughter-in-law, and her loyalty to her.

THE PURPOSE OF GOD FULLFILLED THROUGH HOSPITALITY

Now the Priest of Midian had seven daughters who came and drew water, to water their father's flock. The shepherds came and drove them away, but Moses stood up for them and helped water their flocks. Moses showed kindness to the girls, therefore their father returned kindness to him. He took Moses into his house where he was fed and restored and was made comfortable. He was given a warm welcome, a home, love, contentment and refreshment from the wilderness. This is Hospitality. Moses was given a wife, his good thing. "He who finds a wife, finds a good thing" (Proverbs 18:22). The gift from God to man is the woman he marries. The purpose of God is being fulfilled and being accomplished in his life (Exod. 2:11-21)

THE RESULT OF HOSPITALITY FOR GOD'S GLORY

The two competing sisters in the Bible: Mary and Martha. One was about connection and the other was about perfection for the cause of Hospitality. Hospitality is all about caring, sharing, loving and serving. Mary invited Jesus into her house, where she served him in a hospitable manner. "Love covers a multitude of sins, for by this shall all men know that you are my disciples if you have love one for another" (1 Peter 4:8). Because God is love, if we love our brother then the love of God is dwelling in our hearts. Love should not only be spoken, but activated in a needful way to entertain strangers. For by doing so, we may never tell who we are entertaining; it might be angels. We are not always saints, but for the grace of God. Therefore, we should visit those who are in prison remembering that we were once chained with sin. "Wherein in time past ye walked according to the course of this world, according to the prince of the power of the air, the spirit that now worketh in the children of disobedience"(Ephesians 2:2). Whatever gift God has blessed us with, we should use it for the working of the Ministry and for the edification of the body of Christ.

Hospitality is an opportunity to Minister Christ and His love to those that are in need. Hospitality should be without grumbling. Knowing that whatever we do, we should do it for the glory of God. God is not unrighteous to forget your labor of love that you have ministered to the saints. The Apostle Peter gave the example of Hospitality; "But the end of all things is at hand: be ye therefore sober, and watch unto prayer. And above all things have fervent charity among yourselves: for charity shall cover a multitude of sins. Use Hospitality, one to another, without grudging that God in all things may be glorified through Jesus Christ, to whom be praise and dominion forever and ever Amen." It is not about you but about others (1 Peter 4:7-9,11).

THE RESULT OF HOSPITALITY THROUGH EVANGELISM

Knowing The True God. Then a woman of Samaria came to draw water and Jesus asked her to give him a drink. The woman then left her water pot and went away into the city and said to the men, " Come, see a man, which told me all things that ever I did: is not this the Christ?" (John 4:7, 28-29).

First, Jesus showed Hospitality to the woman by giving her everlasting water which she drank and was satisfied. Her thirst was quenched. Her sins were forgiven; she was all excited with joy and contentment. She just could not keep it to herself. She ran to the village and said, " Come, see a man, which told me all things that ever I did" (John 4:29). His love is overwhelming, affectionate, kind and merciful, forgiving and caring. So different from all the other men that I had in my life. They took advantage of me, abused me and left me sorrowful with shame and regret. But "This Man!," the Lord Jesus, the God of Heaven and Earth, the King of Glory, the Messiah - He made a difference in my life. He shall liberate you; you must come and see Him. For "This Man!" the entire village came. He alone can give you joy and peace, a blessed hope and a bright future.

Naomi taught Ruth how to love, how to be obedient, and how to be respectful to her husband. She was taught how to fear and trust God. Naomi's love for God motivated Ruth to say with intention: "Your God will be my God. Your people will be my people. Where you lodge, I will lodge. The Lord do so between me and you even also, if any but death parts you and me " (Ruth 1:16-17).

Naomi was not concerned about herself. Her concern was for her two daughters-in-law. Hospitality is not about one's self but about others. Jesus said, " For even the Son of man came not to be ministered unto, but to minister, and to give his life a ransom for many." (Mark 10:45). Because of Naomi's awareness of Ruth's needs, God blessed her. She become the grandmother of Obed from whom came our Lord Jesus Christ; who meant so much more to Naomi than ten sons could ever be, allowing the purpose of God to be fulfilled in Ruth's life.

Titus admonishes older women to teach the younger women to be good housewives, to put God first, then their family, then the church. Love your children, spend time with them, and train them up in the fear and admonishment of the Lord. Older women should teach the younger women to love, respect, and be submissive to their husbands. There will be less divorce and abortion if these principles are being emphasized in the Body of Christ by older women. Older women must show Hospitality to younger women by teaching them how to have self-control, how to be temperate, how to maintain their integrity, and how not to be blasphemers but to be encouragers instead; to use kind words with grace, their speech seasoned with salt that minister to the hearers.

Dorcas, a disciple from Joppa, in Acts 9:36 was restored to life due to her Hospitality to her community. Dorcas was full of good works and charitable deeds. "And above all things have fervent charity among yourselves: for charity covers a multitude of sins. Using hospitality one to another without grudging" (1 Peter 4: 8-9). As in the example of

Hospitality in Luke 10:33,35: " But a certain Samaritan, as he journeyed, came where he was: and when he saw him, he had compassion on him, and on the morrow when he departed, he took out two pence, and gave them to the host, and said unto him, 'Take care of him; and whatsoever thou spendest more, when I come again, I will repay thee.'

Mary showed Hospitality through worship. Mary was connected with heavenly things while her sister Martha was concerned about serving in earthly matters. Mary's attention was the only thing that was needful; and that was spending time with the Lord. The things of this world are attractive and can cause us to lose focus. But Mary stayed steadfast, worshipping and praising God.

WOMEN MINISTER THROUGH HOSPITALITY

Throughout scripture we see Hospitality being emphasized. Women advanced Jesus' ministry through their acts of Hospitality.

Hospitality to the prophet: The woman said: "Let us make a little chamber, I pray thee, on the wall; and let us set for him there a bed, and a table, and a stool, and a candlestick: and it shall be, when he cometh to us that he shall turn in thither " (2 Kings 4:10). Because we have showed him kindness.

Kindness to the poor: "She stretcheth out her hand to the poor; yea she reacheth forth her hands to the needy" (Proverbs 31:20). She was not only concerned about herself but she was concerned about the poor and needy. Distributing to saints

Contributing to Christ's Comfort: "And many women were there beholding afar off, which followed Jesus from Galilee, ministering unto him: among which was Mary Magdalene and Mary the mother of James and Joses, and the mother of Zebedee's children" (Matthew 27:55-56). The women were there giving support and bringing comfort to Jesus.

Anointing Christ: "And being in Bethany, in the house of Simon the leper, as he sat at meat, there came a woman having an alabaster box of ointment of spikenard: very precious; and she brake the box, and poured it on his head" (Mark. 14:3). She did not care how much the ointment cost. All she wanted to do was show Hospitality to her Savior.

Washing the Savior's Feet: "And, behold, a woman in the city, which was a sinner, when she knew that Jesus sat at meat in the Pharisee's house, brought an alabaster box of ointment. And stood at his feet behind him weeping, and began to wash his feet with tears, and did wipe them with the hairs of her head, and kissed his feet, and anointed them with the ointment"(Luke 7:37-38).

Serving the Church: "I commend unto you Phebe our sister, which is a servant of the church which is at Cenchrea; That ye receive her in the Lord, as becometh saints, and that ye assist her in whatsoever business she hath need of you: for she hath been a succourer of many, and of myself also" (Romans 16:1-2). Phebe was very helpful to Paul, even took the gospel to Rome for him. She did not mind losing her life because she would find it again. Her propensity was caring for others and hearing the word of God. For she knew that the only way to salvation was through the Lord Jesus Christ and there was power in his word.

Co-laborers with Paul: "Greet Priscilla and Aquila, my helpers in Christ Jesus: Greet Mary, who bestowed much labor on us. Salute Trephena and Tryphosa, who labor in the Lord. Salute the beloved Persis, which labored much in the Lord" (Rom. 16:3,6,12).

Paul had many helpers who were hospitable in the ministry. They labored, they gave their money, and gave their time and their talent to help him propagate the gospel of salvation and thereby fulfilling his destiny in the Lord.

THE SOVEREIGNTY OF GOD THROUGH HOSPITALITY

The Foreknowledge of God: God in eternity past to fulfill His sovereign purpose on this earth. (Nelson's Illustrated Dictionary). He calls individuals to serve Him in spiritual ministries, according to His sovereign will. He calls sinners to repentance and salvation according to His sovereign grace (Ephesians 2:8-10). "H e hath chosen us in him before the foundation of the world" (Ephesians 1:4). God has chosen us and called us to salvation by His Gracious Hospitality. Grace is God's unmerited favor. We are not called upon to decide whether God has chosen us. The responsibility is ours to respond affirmatively to His free offer of salvation in Christ Jesus.

JUSTIFICATION: "He also justifies." Foreknowledge, Predestination, and Calling precede Justification. To be justified is to be declared righteous by God through faith in the victorious death, burial, and bodily resurrection of God's only begotten Son, the Lord Jesus Christ (1 Corinthians 15:1-4). He calls the sinner to salvation by his sovereign grace. The sinner answers the call by faith. Then God judicially declares the sinner righteous, whom He elected or chose according to His foreknowledge.

GLORIFICATION: "He also glorifies." Foreknowledge, Predestination, Calling, and Justification precede Glorification.

Glorification of the saved will complete the sinners' redemption; Christ died to save the whole man: - spirit, soul and body (1 Thessalonians 5:23). Our salvation will not be completed until Jesus returns to this earth, raptures the saved, and glorifies their bodies. John tells us, "We know that when he shall appear, we shall be like Him, for we shall see Him as He is" (1 John 3: 2). All believers will be glorified when Jesus comes. When we see our God and Savior Jesus Christ in His glorified body, "we shall be like Him." Our new bodies will be like His eternal glorious body but with one difference. His glorified body will bear the scars of Calvary forever; ours will not.

THE MINISTRY OF THE HOLY SPIRIT-OUR COMFORTER, OUR HELPER

"And I will pray the Father, and He shall give you another Comforter, that he may abide with you for ever" (John 14:16).

Paraclete is a Greek word used four times in the gospel. It means one who comes alongside to take the place of Jesus. Jesus had to go away for the Comforter to come. The Lord Jesus was the first helper sent by God. He will give you another helper. Now the father will give the disciples the Holy Spirit to help them and all believers; to be with them in the absence of Jesus.

The disciples were sorrowing because Jesus told them that He would go away and they could not go with Him then. They had been with him for thirty years; they had that bonding relationship with Him. They were growing to love Him and implement the teachings he had imparted in them. But the sympathizing Jesus would not leave them comfortless.

He said, "Let not your heart be troubled: ye believed in God, believe also in me. In my Father's house are many mansions: if it were not so, I would have told you. I go to prepare a place for you. And if I go to prepare a place for you, I will come again, and receive you unto myself; that where I am there ye may be also" (John 14:1-3).

"The helper will abide in you forever and will be in you. Let this comfort you in these days of trials and tribulations"(John 14:16). Paul said, "And not only so, but we glory in tribulations also: knowing that tribulation worketh patience; and patience, experience; and experience, hope: and hope maketh not ashamed; because the love of God is shed abroad in our hearts by the Holy Ghost which is given unto us" (Romans 5: 3-5).

The helper has been given to all believers to fill our hearts with the love of God. In this day and age of stress, perplexity, poverty, distress, oppression, and sin, we do need the comfort of the Holy Spirit more than before to empower us to be hospitable to each other.

The Holy Spirit was sent by the Father to glorify Jesus, to take his place, and to continue to teach his disciples all things. He would also cause them to remember all that Jesus taught them, so that they could give us the complete word of God (John 14:26). "To them it was revealed that, not to themselves only but to us also. They were ministering the things which now have been reported to you through those who have preached the gospel to you by the Holy Spirit sent from heaven. Things which angels desire to look upon have been revealed to the saints of God" (1 Peter 1:12).

"But when the Comforter is come, whom I will send unto you from the Father, even the Spirit of truth, which proceedeth from the Father, he shall testify of me:" (John 15: 26). For almost two thousand years the Holy Spirit has motivated believers to give testimony about the saving power of the Lord Jesus Christ (Acts 8:29-40). And the helper will continue to feed obedient servants with the power to share their faith with the lost. Nevertheless, sin is increasing and the love of many is waxing cold. But the power of the Holy Spirit will illuminate believers to preach the good tidings, to preach the gospel of salvation, and to declare that Jesus is the answer Jesus is the way! Jesus is the truth! Jesus is the light!

In those last and closing days, believers need to be empowered by the Holy Spirit to propagate the gospel of Salvation. This is the time to hold up the bloodstained banner, to cry aloud, to spare not and to show the people their salvation. Point them to Christ to prepare them for eternity. If there ever was a time, it's now! Therefore, we need to open our doors of Hospitality. For Jesus is soon to return. "For the Lord himself shall descend from heaven with a shout, with the voice of the archangel, and with the trump of God: and the dead in Christ shall rise first: then we which are alive and remain shall be caught up together with them in the clouds, to meet the Lord in the air: and so shall we ever be with the Lord. Wherefore comfort one another with these words" (1 Thessalonians 4:16-18).

LOVE ACCORDING TO THE BIBLE (KJV)

For God so loved the world (sinful men, His creation), "that he gave his only begotten Son, that whosoever believeth in him should not perish, but have everlasting life" (John 3:16). The greatest love story ever written. God's unconditional love for us. He sent His only son to die on the cross to redeem us to Him. Love is the highest esteem God has for His human children and it is the highest regard they should have for Him in return as His people. There are hundreds of references to love in the Bible. One of them is: "Greater love has no man than this, that a man lay down His life for a friend." Therefore, we are confident that all our sins are forgiven. We can cast all our cares upon Him, for He cares for us. The Bible is certainly the most remarkable book of love in the world: "Herein is love, not that we loved God, but that he loved us, and sent his Son to be the propitiation for our sins." (1 John 4:10). The Apostle Paul said that, "Christ Jesus came into the world to save sinners of whom he was chief."

Love is not only an attribute of God: it is also an essential part of His nature. "God is love," the Bible declares in 1 John 4:8-16. Love is the personification of God. Such love surpasses our power of understanding (Ephesians 3:19).

Love like this is everlasting (Jeremiah 31:3), free (Hosea 14:4), sacrificial (John 3:16), and enduring to the end (John 13:1). It is stated that it was not the nails that kept Jesus on the cross but His great love for us.

Two distinct Greek words for love appear in the Bible. The word 'phileo' means "to have ardent affection and feelings" or "brotherly love", which is a type of impulsive love. The word 'agape' means "to have esteem" or "highest regard", it is the highest form of love. Jesus was hospitable to Peter. He took time to dine with him. "So when they had dined, Jesus saith to Simon Peter, 'Simon, Son of Jonas, lovest thou me more than these?' He said unto him, 'Yea Lord; thou knowest that I love thee.' He saith unto him, 'Feed my lambs.'" In this memorable conversation between Jesus and Peter, Jesus was testing Peter's love for Him (John 21:15-17). Jesus asked, "Simon, do you love [esteem] me?" But Peter replied, "You know that I love you [have ardent affection for you]." Then Jesus asked again, "Simon, do you love me, have ardent affection for me?" Jesus wanted Peter to prove his love for Him by feeding His sheep.

Peter's love was agape love, which means a love that held Jesus in highest esteem above all else. The word agape is the characteristic expression of Christianity. This word for love is used in several different ways in the Bible.

1. Agape love indicates the nature of the love of God towards His beloved Son (John 17:26), towards the human race generally (John 3:16; Romans 5:8), and toward those who believe in the Lord Jesus Christ (John 14:21).

2. Agape love conveys God's will for His children about their attitude towards one another. Love for one another was the proof to the world. The true disciples of Jesus Christ will

demonstrate Hospitality: "By this shall men know that ye are my disciples" (John 13: 35).

Love According to the Bible (KJV)

3. Agape love also expresses the essential nature of God (1 John 4:8). Love can be known only from the actions it prompts, as seen in God's love in the gift of His Son (1 John 4:9-10). Love found its perfect expression in the Lord Jesus. Christian love is the fruit of the Spirit of Jesus in the believer (Galatians 5:22). Love is like oil (Nelsons Dictionary) to the wheels of obedience. It enables us to run the way of God's commandments (Psalm 119:32). Without such love, we are nothing (1 Corinthians 13:3). Such Spirit-inspired love never fails (1 Corinthians 13:8) but always flourishes and motivates to share Hospitality.

4. Brotherly love: what does that mean? Love of others or each other (Romans 12:10; Hebrews 13:1; 2 Peter 1:7); this phrase is used in a symbolic sense to express love of Christians for one another, since all are the sons of the same Father. The Greek word translated as brotherly love implies more than love for one's "blood brother", as in the secular writings; it also means love for a brotherhood of the true believers, for the members of the church, the "household of faith" (Galatians 6:10) and "of God" (Ephesians 2:19; also 1 Peter 2:17; 3:8; 5:9).

Christians are a brotherhood in the service of Christ; which are united by the blood of Christ (Matthew 23:8); a family made up of those who do the will of God. And it is God's will that we show Hospitality, one to another (Matthew 12:50; Mark 3:35; Luke 8:21). "A new commandment I give unto you," Jesus said to His disciples, "That ye love one another. By this shall all men know that ye are my disciples, if ye have love one to another" (John 13:34-35).

PRAYER IS THE NUCLEUS OF HOSPITALITY:

According to the Nelson's Illustrated Bible Dictionary, prayer is communication with God. And because God is personal, all people can offer prayers. However, sinners who have not trusted Jesus Christ for their salvation remain alienated from God. So while unbelievers may pray, they do not have the basis for a rewarding fellowship with God. They have not met the conditions laid down in the Bible for effectiveness in prayer.

Christians recognize their dependence upon their Creator. They have reason to express gratitude for God's blessings. But they have far more reasons to respond to God than this. They respond to the love of God for them. God's love is revealed through the marvelous incarnation and life of Christ, His atoning provision at the cross, His resurrection, as well as His continuing presence through the Holy Spirit. Prayer is not a method of showing Hospitality; Prayer is the Ministry of Hospitality. "For the eyes of the Lord are over the righteous, and his ears are open unto their prayers" (1 Peter 3:12). Prayer meets us on his behalf. And the Lord opened the prison door and released Peter from prison (Acts 12:5-10). Prayer cannot be replaced by devout good works in a needy world. As important as service to others is, at times we must turn away from it to God, who is distinct from all things and over all things. Neither should prayer be thought of as a mystical experience in which people lose their identity in the infinite reality. Effective prayer must be a scripturally informed response of persons saved by grace to the living God, who can hear and answer on the basis of Christ's payment of the penalty which sinners deserved. As such, prayer involves several important aspects.

1. **FAITH:** The most meaningful prayer comes from a heart that places its trust in God who has acted and spoken in Jesus, and the teachings of the Bible. God spoke to us through the Bible, and we in turn, speak to Him in trustful believing prayer. Assured by the scripture that God is personal, living, active, all-knowing, all-wise, and all-powerful, we know that God can hear and help us. A confident prayer life is built on the cornerstone of Christ's work and words as shown by the prophets and apostles in the Sprit-inspired writings of the Bible.

2. **WORSHIP:** In worship, we recognize what is of highest worth- not ourselves, others, or our work, but God. Only the highest divine being deserves our highest respect. Guided by scripture, we set our values in accordance with God's will and perfect standards. Before God, angels hide their faces and cry, "Holy, Holy, Holy is the Lord of hosts" (Isaiah 6:3). The angels could not sing amazing grace; for they never knew the joy that saved them by grace. Only we can sing "amazing grace, how sweet the sound that saved a wretch like me...." Because of His grace we are to show Hospitality in worship to our Lord.

3. **CONFESSION:** Awareness of God's holiness leads to confession of our own sinfulness. Like the prophet Isaiah, he exclaimed, "Woe is me, for I am undone; because I am

a man of unclean lips, and I dwell in the midst of a people of unclean lips: for mine eyes have seen the King, the Lord of hosts" (Isaiah 6:5). By sinning, we hurt ourselves and those closest to us. But first of all and worst of all, sin is against God (Psalm 51:4), we must confess to God to get right with Him. We need not confess them to another being but we should confess them directly to God, who promises to forgive us of all our unrighteousness (1 John 1:9). However we need to reconcile to those we have offended and make amends. In the Bible, iniquity in the heart (Psalm 66:18) is refusal to hear Gods' love. It is certain in the most remarkable book in the world, the Bible: here is love, not that we love God but that he loves us and sent his Son to be a propitiation for our sins.

Love is not the only attribute; it is also an essential part of God's nature. God is love, the Bible declares (1 John 4:16) and Jesus is the personification of God's love. Such love surpasses our power of understanding (Ephesians 3:19). Love like this is everlasting (Jeremiah 31:3). Love will free you (Hosea 14:4); sacrificial and enduring to the end.

4. **ADORATION:** God is love, and he has demonstrated His love in the gift of His Son. The greatest desire of God is that we love Him with our whole being (Matthew 22:37). Our love should be expressed, as His has been expressed, in both deeds and words. People sometimes find it difficult to say to others and to God, "I love you." But when love for God fills our lives, we will express our love in prayer to the one who is ultimately responsible for all that we are.

5. **PRAISE:** The natural outgrowth of faith, worship, confession and adoration is praise. We speak well of one we highly esteem and love. The one whom we respect and love above all others naturally receives the highest commendation. We praise Him for His

   The Ministry of Hospitality "mighty acts: praise him according to His excellent greatness!" (Psalm 150:2), and for His "righteous judgments" (Psalm 119:164). For God Himself, for His works, and for His words, His people give sincere praise.

6. **THANSKGIVING:** There are many people who are not thankful because they have not received what they think is due to them. But if we got what we "deserved" we would be condemned because of our guilt. As sinners, we are not people of God by nature. We have no claim upon His mercy and grace. Nevertheless, He has forgiven our sins and granted us acceptance as His people. He has given us His righteous standing and a new heart and life. Ingratitude marks the ungodly (Romans 1:21). Believers, in contrast, live thankfully. God has been at work on our behalf in countless ways. So in everything, even for the discipline that is unpleasant, we give thanks (Colossians 3:17; 1 Thessalonians 5:18).

7. **DEDICATED ACTION:** Christ's example does not require us to withdraw from society, but to render service to the needy in a spirit of prayer. He wept over Jerusalem in compassionate prayer, and then He went into the city to give His life as a ransom for many. Authentic prayer will

be the source of courage and productivity, as it was for the prophets and apostles.

8. **REQUEST:** Prayer is not only a response to God's grace as brought to us in the life and work of Jesus and the teaching of scripture; it is also a requisition form for our needs and the needs of others. For good reason, God's holy and wise purpose does not permit Him to grant every portion just as we asked. Several hindrances to answered prayer are mentioned in the Bible: iniquity in the heart (Psalm 66:18), refusal to hear God's law (Proverbs 28:9), an estranged heart (Isaiah 29:13), sinful separation from God (Isaiah 59:2), waywardness (Jeremiah 14:10-12), offering unworthy sacrifices (Malachi1:7-9), praying to be seen by men (Matthew 6:5-6), pride in fasting and tithing (Luke 18:11-14), lack of faith (Hebrews 11:6), and doubting or double-mindedness (James 4:3).

More positively, God has promised to answer our requests when we start helping the hungry and the afflicted (Isaiah 58:9-10), when we believe that we will receive what we ask for (Mark 11:22-24), when we forgive others (Mark 11:25-26), when we abide in Christ and His words, when we pray in the Spirit (Ephesians 6:8), and when we obey the Lord's commandments (1 John 5:14-15). Until we have properly responded to God and His Word, He cannot entrust us with His powerful resources.

Prayer is a request to a personal Lord who answers as He knows best. We should not think that we will always have success in obtaining the things for which we ask. In His wisdom, God hears and answers in the way that is best.

9. **EFFECTIVENESS:** Prayer has power over everything. God can intelligently act in any part of the universe or human history. Although some people think that prayer is a waste of time, the Bible declares that " The effectual fervent prayer of a righteous man availeth much" (James 5:16). Prayer meets inner needs. One who prays will receive freedom from fear, fruitfulness, endurance, patience and joy (Colossians 1:9-12), quiet satisfaction (Isaiah 58:9-11), wisdom and understanding (Daniel 9:20-27), deliverance from harm (Joel 2:32), rewards (Matthew 6:6), good gifts (Luke 11:13), fullness of joy (John 16:23-24), peace (Philippians 4:6-8), and freedom from anxiety (1 Peter 5:7).

Is prayer effective only in the inner lives of those who pray? No! Prayer can make a difference in the lives of others too.

Biblical writers believed prayer for others could result in greater wisdom and power (Ephesians 1:18-19), inward strength, knowledge of Christ's love, filling with God's fullness (Ephesians 3:16-19), discernment, approval of what is excellent, filling with the fruits of righteousness (PhilIppians 1:9-11), knowledge of God's will, spiritual understanding, a life pleasing to God, fruitfulness, endurance, patience, joy (Colossians 1:9-12), a quiet peaceable life (1 Timothy 2:1-2), love for others and all people, holiness before God, steadfastness in Christ (2 Thessalonians 3:5), the sharing of one's faith, promotion of the knowledge of all that is good (Philemon 6), and equipment for every good work that is pleasing to God (Hebrews 13:20-21).

Some people who think prayer can affect others often question the ability of God to change His usual patterns in the physical world. But some prayers in the Bible changed nature and physical bodies. Jabez prayed for enlarged borders and protection from harm (1 Chronicles 4:10). Other people in the Bible prayed for deliverance from trouble (Psalm 34:15-22), deliverance from both poverty and riches (Proverbs 30:7-9), and deliverance from the belly of a great fish (Jonah 2:7-10). Some prayed for daily bread (Matthew 6:11), for preservation and sanctification of spirit, soul, and body (1 Thessalonians 5:23), for the healing of the sick (James 5:14-15), and for the end of the rain and its beginning again (James 5:17-18).

When the disciples prayed, the building around them shook (Acts 4:31) and an earthquake opened the doors of their prison (Acts 16.25-26). Our prayers do make a difference in how God acts in the world.

HOSPITALITY THROUGH COUNSELING

For unto us a child is born, unto us a son is given: and the government shall be upon his shoulder: and his name will be called Wonderful, Counsellor, The mighty God, The everlasting Father, The Prince of Peace. Of the increase of his government and peace there shall be no end" (Isaiah9:6-7). Counseling answers people's questions, restores broken lives, reconciles families, gives hope to the hopeless and changes lives for life and eternity.

People pay large sums of money to attorneys, psychiatrists and psychologist for counseling, but they fail to realize that Jesus is the true Counselor who charges no fees and His counsel is sound and enduring. Jesus is the Wonderful Counselor. He meets us at the lowest point in life and restores us to the highest level. He is "great in counsel, and mighty in work: for thine eyes are open upon the ways of the sons of men: to give every one according to his ways, and according to the fruit of his doings"(Jeremiah 32:19). His hands are outstretched to pick us up when we fall. "The steps of a good man are ordered by the Lord: and he delighteth in his way. Though he fall, he shall not be utterly cast down: for the Lord upholdeth him with his hand" (Psalm. 37:23-24).

God is a good Father who pitieth His children. He knows what is best for us even though we do not understand his ways: God has only good plans for his children. "For my thoughts are not your thoughts, neither are your ways my ways,' saith the Lord. 'For as the heavens are higher than the earth, so are my ways higher than your ways, and thoughts than your thoughts'" (Isaiah 55:8-9).

THE NEED FOR COUNSELING

Counseling deals with individuals with unique needs, thoughts, and behaviors. Therefore, each case must be treated exclusively with expected individual results and answers - Counselor Evert L. Worthington Jr.

We are a needy people. We need God at the center of our lives, though some people do not yet know this. God created us with a fundamental yearning for permanent, intimate and productive fellowship with Him. Our natures reflect this need. God created man to be counseled by Him. But the problem with human beings is that they reject God's counseling for what the devil has to offer.

We experience a direct yearning for God, knowing that there must be more to life than daily existence. We desire the beautiful, the sublime, the more-to-life than daily existence. We will experience success when we acknowledge God in all our ways. "Trust in the Lord with all thy heart; and lean not unto your own understanding. In all thy ways acknowledge him, and he shall direct thy paths" (Proverbs 3:5-6)

"If we walk in the light, as He is in the light, we have fellowship one with another, and the blood of Jesus Christ his Son, cleanseth us from all sin" (1 John 1:7). We want to do constructive things with our lives. We want to be prolific citizens while here on earth and also gain eternal life in heaven. We often act on earth consistently with how God created us to act forever. "Beloved, I wish above all things that thou mayest prosper and be in health, even as thy soul prospereth" (3 John 1:2).

We experience an indirect need for God, too. Because God created us with His nature stamped upon us in His image and likeness, we strive to fulfill yearnings for permanence, intimacy, and productivity in our relationships with other people. Through intimacy and work we achieve a sense of meaning that reaches its completeness in our eternal relationship with God through Jesus Christ our Redeemer.

But, in today's world, we substitute relationship with God with the works of the flesh: adultery, fornication, uncleanness, lasciviousness, idolatry, sorcery, hatred, strife, jealousy, wrath, envy, murder, and drunkenness; as well as desire power and influence, rather than the will, the purpose and the plan of God which is good and acceptable and perfect for our lives.

These substitutions constitute sin in our lives and lead to hurt and blame. Sometimes the consequences are greater than the actions which lead to estrangement from God and people. We need God's forgiveness for rebelling against His laws, we also need forgiveness from others and reconciliation with those we have hurt.

"But my God shall supply all your needs according to his riches in glory by Christ Jesus" (Philippians 4:19). As with all needs, God fills our needs for forgiveness and heals hurt and blame when we turn to Him rather than away from Him. Nevertheless, we also need forgiveness from others, and we need to forgive others who have hurt us. God is gracious. He is able to make all grace abound towards us and He can help us forgive others by following His example and His initiative. One of the last words of Jesus before His death was, "Father forgive them; for they know not what they do. And they parted His raiment, and cast lots " (Luke 23:34).

HOSPITALITY AND KINDNESS

The world that we are living in today is so very busy. People are always rushing to do something or to go somewhere. People are depressed and stressed out, worried about losing their jobs and homes. People have little time for a word of kindness or acts of kindness. But there are some special people who are dedicated to showing kindness to others. These people are called by God to be hospitable to those who are forgotten by this world's demands.

Some people do not even know their next-door neighbors. They feel overextended and rushed to the limit for their own portion of the cares of life; there is no time for others. Still, there are dedicated special people with a propensity to show kindness to others. These people do not allow their deadlines or their demanding schedules to hinder their acts of Hospitality.

These special faithful people are there whenever the need arises, whenever the call is made for comfort and encouragement, or to a give a drink of cold water. Jesus said " inasmuch as ye have done it unto one of the least of these my brethren, ye have done it unto me" (Matthew 25:40) to rescue those snared in traps. By showing kindness to someone could mean a difference for life and eternity. Kindness and Hospitality are correlated. The psalmist said, "Thy lovingkindness is better than life, my lips shall praise thee. Thus I will bless thee while I live: I will lift up my hands in thy name. My soul shall be satisfied as with marrow and fatness ; and my mouth shall praise thee with joyful lips" (Psalm 63:3-5).

When King David was in the wilderness of Judah, he missed the fellowship he had with God in the sanctuary.

He considered himself as being thirsty in a dry land where there was no water. Therefore, he would seek the Lord early in the morning to be strengthened, to be refreshed and to experience the power and glory of God as he used to experience in the sanctuary. God would satisfy his soul with joy and comfort him with peace and shield him from the sneers of his enemies,

God was hospitable to David in his wilderness experience, being pursued by his enemies. Hospitality is the ministry of helping people to resolve their problems and afflictions in accordance to the teachings of the Bible. He that is strong must "Bear ye one another's burdens, and so fulfil the law of Christ. " (Galatians 6:2). Hospitality is my propensity to intercede and be a supplicant on behalf of others.

During his voyage to Rome, the Apostle Paul became very ill and Julius, a centurion of Augustus, treated him kindly. He nursed him, and made sure that he was free to visit his friends, engage in fellowship and preach the gospel (Acts 27:3).

A story is told of a young man who could not find a room in a hotel because of the location he had traveled from. He became very depressed and abandoned. The hotel receptionist felt his pain and showed empathy by taking him to his own house for the night. What do you call this? It is Hospitality and lovingkindness in action.

Naomi was not only a godly woman; she was also a kindhearted woman. She was solicitous about Ruth's future. She instructed Ruth on how to present herself before Boaz. And Ruth did exactly what her mother-in-law told her to do. Older women must "teach the young women to be sober, to love their husbands, to love their children, to be discreet, chaste, keepers at home, good, obedient to their own husbands, that the word of God be not blasphemed" (Titus 2:4-5). If there were older women mentors, there would be less divorce and abortions. Childhood obesity would be lower because younger mothers would be taught to cook more home meals for their children. This rings true in Naomi's words to her daughter-in-law, Ruth, when she was advising her on how to get her husband: "When he lieth down, that thou shalt mark the place where he shall lie, and thou shalt go in, and uncover his feet, and lay thee down; and he will tell thee what thou shalt do" (Ruth 3:4).

Ruth was always obedient to her mother-in-law. She treated her with respect and honor and her mother-in-law returned kindness to her. I highly recommend Ruth's love story. It is a model for young women to emulate. Ruth did not sleep with the man, but uncovered his feet, and lay down. When Boaz awoke he saw the young woman lying at his feet and because she was hospitable to him, he in return showed her kindness. Then he said, " Blessed be thou of the Lord, my daughter: for thou hast shewed more kindness in the latter end than at the beginning, inasmuch as thou followedst not young men, whether poor or rich. And now, my daughter, fear not; I will do to thee all that thou requirest: for all the city of my people doth know that thou art a virtuous woman" (Ruth 3:10-11). And a virtuous woman is hospitable.

Jonathan shows Hospitality to David: David and Jonathan were very good friends. When King Saul, Jonathan's father was pursuing David to kill him because of jealousy, Jonathan was his defense. He protected David on numerous occasions from his father's misguided wrath. After King Saul's death, David fulfilled his anointed destiny of becoming king of Israel, administering judgment and justice to all his people. When David's Kingship was established, Jonathan was already dead. However, David wanted to return the kind deeds Jonathan had bestowed upon him. So he requested that Mephibosheth, the son of Jonathan, the grandson of Saul be brought to him. He was hospitable to him. David said to him, "Fear not: for I will surely shew thee kindness for Jonathan thy father's sake, and will restore to thee all the land of Saul thy father; and thou shalt eat bread at my table continually" (2 Samuel 9:7).

David prayed with confidence because God had shown him His lovingkindness by His right hand. David had experienced God's divine protection and deliverance from his enemies many, many times. He was persuaded that whatever he would ask God for in prayer it would be granted unto him. Prayer was David's source of strength and power in his everyday life. Therefore, he was confident in saying, "I have called upon thee, for thou wilt hear me, O God: incline thine ear unto me, and hear my speech. Shew thy marvellous lovingkindness, O thou that savest by thy right hand, them which put their trust in thee from those that rise up against them. " (Psalm 17:6-7).

God loved Israel with an everlasting love. God Himself declared that His love for the nation of Israel is everlasting despite the fact that He has judged that nation. He looks beyond our faults and bestows His love upon us. " Behold, what manner of love the Father hath bestowed upon us, that we should be called the sons of God. Greater love hath no man than this, that a man lay down his life for a friends" (1 John 3:1, John 15:13). God is a merciful, kind, compassionate and long-suffering Father. It does not matter how far away we may stray from Him. His loving arms are still outstretched to bring us into the fold. 'The Lord hath appeared of old unto me, saying, 'Yea, I have loved thee with an everlasting love: therefore with lovingkindness have I drawn thee'" (Jeremiah 31:3).

The woman of Proverb 31 was a wise woman who knew how to bridle her tongue and how to give a word of wisdom to those who were without. Her speech was with grace, seasoned with salt, that ministered to her hearers; a word of comfort, or hope to those who were overwhelmed, discouraged, perplexed and bewildered. The word of hope should never be underestimated. It can bring about change to those who are in difficult situations. In times of hopelessness, we can take comfort in the Word of God. The fruits of hope according to June Hunt, in "How to Rise above Abuse", are as follows:

1. Hope produces joy that remains even through the most difficult trials (Proverbs 10:28).

2. Hope produces perseverance (Romans 8:24-25).

3. Hope produces confidence (2 Corinthians 3:12).

4. Hope produces ministry (2 Corinthians 4:8-18).

5. Hope produces greater love and faith (Colossians 1:4-5).

6. Hope produces consistency (1 Thessalonians 1:3).

7. Hope produces increased energy and enthusiasm (1 Timothy 4:10).

8. Hope produces stability (Hebrews 6:19).

9. Hope produces a more intimate relationship with God (Hebrews 7:19).

10. Hope produces personal purity (1 John 3:3).

The woman of Proverbs 31 knew that a soft answer turns away wrath. "Let the word of Christ dwell in you richly in all wisdom; teaching and admonishing one another, in psalms and hymns and spiritual songs, singing with grace in your hearts to the Lord" (Colossians 3:16). This was her way of showing kindness. "She openeth her mouth with wisdom; and in her tongue is the law of kindness" (Proverbs 31:26).

This is an era of depression, oppression, despair and anxiety. People need hope, confidence, faith and belief in the One True and Living God who cannot fail; who is sure, steadfast and unchangeable. He has the ability, capability, and, authority to do abundantly above all we ask or think. "For with God nothing shall be impossible" (Luke 1:37). People are looking for change, which can only be found in those who hospitably give that blessed hope. There is also false hope, which is based on human perceptions of what is pleasurable and desirable-it's about getting what you want. False hope is based on denial of reality. It begins in the mind. Therefore, the mind must be changed. "For as he thinketh in his heart, so is he: Eat and drink, saith he to thee, but his heart is not with thee" (Proverbs 23:7).

Paul was well aware of the battle of the mind; so he admonished the believers to transform their mind to that of Christ. "And be not conformed to this world: but be ye transformed by the renewing of your mind, that ye may prove what is that good, and acceptable, and perfect, will of God" (Romans 12:2). There is also true Hope, based on the promises of God. Abraham experienced that true Hope in the promise of God, which he later put into action in the form of Hospitality to the strangers who came to his house.

Abraham was confident that the God who promised, was the "Omnipotent One" who was able to keep his promise. "Who against hope believed in hope, that he might become the father of many nations, according to that which was spoken, so shall thy seed be" (Romans 4:18). The Apostle Peter also admonished us to experience the promises of God given to us through hope, that we can demonstrate Hospitality in brotherly kindness, godliness and charity. Charity enables us to help the fallen brother, to visit the widow and the fatherless, to give to the necessity of the saints and to care for the poor. "Whereby are given unto us exceeding great and precious promises: that by these ye might be partakers of the divine nature, having escaped the corruption that is in the world through lust. And beside this, giving all diligence, add to your faith virtue; and to virtue knowledge; and to knowledge temperance, and to temperance patience; and to patience godliness; and to godliness brotherly kindness; and to brotherly kindness charity."(2Peter 1:4-7).

Through these promises we can demonstrate the ministry of Hospitality. True Hope remains steadfast in the vision. The Apostle Paul was a perfect example of a steadfast visionary to the call of Christ. Paul's Hope was not in his trials or persecutions but in the plan and purpose of God to propagate the gospel to the Gentiles; and to be an instrument to build, nurture and edify the body of Christ. Paul was an excellent teacher in promoting Hospitality in the church. "But I would ye should understand, brethren, that the things which happened unto me have fallen out rather unto the furtherance of the gospel; So that my bonds in Christ are manifest in all the palace, and in all other places;

and many brethren in the Lord, waxing confident by my bonds, are much more bold to speak the word without fear" (Philippians 1:12-14). The Apostle Paul was passionate about the ministry of Hospitality. He motivated the saints to be kind one to another, to forgive one another, and to help the weaker brother. To be consistent in well doing, for in due season we shall reap if we do not become faint. "Brethren, if a man be overtaken in a fault, ye which are spiritual, restore such a one in the spirit of meekness; considering thyself, lest thou also be tempted. Bear ye one another's burdens, and so fulfil the law of Christ" (Galatians 6:1-2). Paul was adamant about Hospitality, that he encouraged the Galatians to seize every opportunity they got to do well unto all men, especially in the household of faith.

Hospitality committee in the church: Pastors must encourage prayer for the vision to continue in the Church. The Hospitality committee is one of the essential parts of the growth of the church. The very first person a visitor sees when entering the church is the usher. Therefore, the usher must be polite, gentle, kind and cheerful in welcoming the guest. If his or her mannerism is unbecoming, the visitor will be turned off and might never return. The church should be the most hospitable place to embrace visitors because people come to church for various reasons. If their needs are not met, they may dislike church or even blame God.

Hospitality is to create a loving atmosphere that draws sinners to Christ, restore broken hearts, give hope to the hopeless, comfort to the distressed, reconciliation of families, counsel and to have fellowship with the lonely.

ABOUT THE AUTHOR

Dr. Joan A. Polidore was born in 1947 to Mr. Cyril and Astashia Dejean on the Caribbean island of Dominica. Joan attended the St. Martin Catholic School and the Morne Prosper Government School. After graduation in 1964, she began teaching as a public school teacher and, in 1970, as a preschool teacher at St. Martin Catholic School. She married Julian Polidore in 1977 and they have four beautiful daughters.

In 1979, Joan Polidore and her husband were forced to relocate to the USA due to the devastation of their island home by hurricane David. Upon arrival in the USA, Joan started attending Gospel Light House Assembly and served as an evangelist, sunday school teacher, choir director and the president of the Women's Ministry.

In 1988, God gave Joan a vision of the children on the streets of Roosevelt and mandated her to establish a foundation and to be the repairer of the breach. When others closed the door on the youth, Joan opened her heart, arms and home to them. She instilled the word of God in them to build their self-worth and empower them to be prolific citizens.

In 1997, Joan became a member of Abundant Life Ministries International, where she was appointed dean of Abundant Life Bible

School and president of the community outreach program and S.A.Y. Save America's Youth (SAY) Yes program. With all this, Joan continued to play an important role in the lives of the young people from Roosevelt. She merged her Roosevelt program with her Hempstead youth group. This move empowered the young people to learn, achieve and make prudent choices.

In 2001, due to continued faithfulness in Jesus Christ, Joan and her husband were called by the Lord to give birth to Agape Christian Academy at 281 Clinton Street, Hempstead. Agape Ministries is a purpose-driven ministry, empowered to prosper and touch the wombs of the weary. Equipped to tear down every stronghold or any giant that might stand against the plan of God, Agape Ministry has been ordained by God to destroy the yokes of bondage over this generation so that our community and culture can move forward and live life in abundance.

The Ministry has expanded to meet the community needs with a bundle of love. The ministry has expanded to serving the community with a food ministry, a food pantry, a youth center, a preschool and a transitional home for the homeless and those rejected by society. She has brought restoration and reconciliation to many families.

Pastor Joan is now an ordained chaplain and acquired her Masters' of Divinity at Southwest Bible College and Seminary in November 2013 and her Doctorate in Christian Counseling in 2015. She has served as an advocate for many young men in Nassau County Correctional Facility and State Prisons also. She is a youth counselor who mentors and counsels unwed mothers. Pastor Joan is a family care provider for the mentally challenged who are in need of daily supervision and emotional support. She is now the resident pastor with her husband of the Warner Pentecostal Church on the island of Dominica in the Caribbean.

"We have seen many lives changed, restored and healed and many are being fed through this ministry. We can sincerely say that the Lord has done great things for us, and it is only because of Him we are here today to celebrate the faithfulness of the Lord, to take this ministry to the next level. We are grateful to all who have supported us in the past.

ACKNOWLEDGEMENT

I am pleased to take this opportunity to thank my colleagues, friends, and faculty members who have helped me with this research project. I am most indebted to my teacher, Sue Joy, who inspired me to explore the Ministry of Hospitality. I would also like to thank my husband Pastor Julian, and my daughter Julia Polidore-Okley, for sharing in this research and helping me. I would like to thank Deacon Russel Bostic for all his help. Finally, I thank all my prayer partners for interceding on my behalf when I was too exhausted to pray.

www.ingramcontent.com/pod-product-compliance
Lightning Source LLC
LaVergne TN
LVHW010615070526
838199LV00063BA/5161